Original title:
Snow-Capped Thoughts

Copyright © 2024 Swan Charm
All rights reserved.

Author: Kaido Väinamäe
ISBN HARDBACK: 978-9916-79-708-2
ISBN PAPERBACK: 978-9916-79-709-9
ISBN EBOOK: 978-9916-79-710-5

Beneath the Icy Surface

In the depths where shadows sway,
Frozen dreams lie still and gray.
Secrets buried, whispers breathe,
Silent hopes beneath the wreath.

Frost-Kissed Ideas

Glimmers of thoughts in icy light,
Fragrant visions, crisp and bright.
Winter's touch on every spark,
Crafting tales beneath the dark.

.

Ethereal Winter Whispers

Gentle breezes weave a tune,
Moonlight dances with the rune.
Snowflakes twirl, soft tales unfold,
Ethereal stories, pure as gold.

Hushed Thoughts Beneath the Drift

Quiet musings slip and slide,
Beneath the layers, secrets hide.
In the stillness, truth resides,
Hushed reflections, winter's guide.

Secret Gardens Beneath the Ice

In winter's hush, the world lies still,
Whispers of life beneath the chill.
Soft petals hide in frozen ground,
Dreaming of spring's gentle sound.

Beneath the frost, the roots entwine,
A hidden realm where colors shine.
Life waits patiently, a silent sigh,
For sunlit days to draw nigh.

Icicles cloak the secrets deep,
In silent slumber, they softly sleep.
Each drop of dew a promise made,
Of blooming beauty soon displayed.

When thaw arrives, the world awakes,
With vibrant hues that nature makes.
In secret gardens, joy takes flight,
Painting a canvas pure and bright.

So trust the hush of winter's reign,
For life persists beneath the pain.
In every frost, a tale untold,
Of gardens waiting to unfold.

A Canvas of Crystal

Upon the dawn's soft light,
A canvas gleams so bright.
Each crystal drop, a prayer,
Whispers of beauty rare.

Silent trees stand tall,
Draped in white, they call.
Nature's art displayed,
In frosty hues, arrayed.

Footprints mark the snow,
Where wandering hearts go.
In this quiet space,
Time slows its frantic pace.

At dusk, the skies ignite,
With shades of pale twilight.
Stars begin to gleam,
Painting winter's dream.

Here, peace finds its way,
In the light of day.
A canvas made of ice,
Where beauty does suffice.

Echoes Beneath the Chill

In the stillness we find,
Echoes of love entwined.
Soft whispers in the air,
Gentle comfort we share.

Beneath the stars' embrace,
Cold winds begin to trace.
Each note a memory,
Wrapped in wintry glee.

The trees sway and bend,
As night begins to mend.
A lullaby of sound,
In the frost, we're found.

Footsteps crunch like glass,
In the quiet, we pass.
Together, side by side,
With the world as our guide.

As dawn breaks the spell,
We'll remember it well.
Beneath the chill we roam,
Finding echoes of home.

Dreams in a Frosty Frame

In dreams of icy nights,
Hope takes its graceful flights.
Framed by shadows long,
The heart begins to throng.

Whispers dance through air,
In the magic laid bare.
Stars twinkle with delight,
Painting dreams in the night.

Each flake, a secret spun,
A tale of hearts begun.
Frosty breaths ignite,
In the calm of our sight.

Through windows hazed with frost,
We ponder what is lost.
Yet warmth lives in each heart,
In the frost, we're a part.

Awake beneath the moon,
We find our own sweet tune.
In a world dressed in white,
Dreams emerge in the night.

The Stillness of Snowfall

As snow begins to fall,
A hush envelops all.
Nature's blanket spreads wide,
Softly, it will abide.

Silent flakes descend,
Their beauty, we commend.
Each one a fleeting grace,
Joining in time and space.

The world takes a pause,
Reflecting without cause.
In the still of the night,
Our hearts feel the light.

Underneath the gray,
Life finds its own way.
In the quiet, we see,
The magic that can be.

With every gentle sigh,
The moments drift and fly.
In snowfall's tender touch,
We find we love it much.

Etched in Ice: Silenced Heartbeats

In the stillness, whispers freeze,
Echoes trapped beneath the snow.
Time pauses, as moments seize,
Silenced heartbeats begin to flow.

Shadows dance in the pale moonlight,
While stars weave dreams on icy beams.
Memories drift, lost from sight,
Captured softly in frozen gleams.

Each breath forms a cloud, a sigh,
Painted gently on winter's breath.
Nature's hush, a quiet cry,
Holds the secrets of life and death.

Branches bow with the weight of years,
Carved by time, the stories told.
Through frost, laughter often clears,
Life's warmth thrives within the cold.

Yet hope flickers in the chill,
A spark that fights the endless night.
Heartbeats echo, loud and still,
In the silence, love takes flight.

Veils of White: A Dreamer's Pause

Snowflakes drift like whispered dreams,
Softly falling, a blanket bright.
In this world, nothing seems,
To rush the tender, tranquil night.

Veils of white weave through the trees,
Hiding secrets of what lies below.
A dreamer's mind drifts with ease,
In this realm, time moves slow.

Footsteps crunch on the powdery floor,
Each sound lingers in the air.
Wonders breathe in a gentle score,
Every heartbeat, a silent prayer.

Moments gather, a timeless space,
Where thoughts collide and hearts explore.
In the stillness, a warm embrace,
With winter's charm, we seek for more.

As dawn breaks, the world alights,
Casting shadows in golden hue.
Yet memories of starry nights,
Stay forever in the heart's view.

Glimmers of Anticipation in the Cold

Frosty air hangs heavy, bright,
Glimmers dance on the frozen ground.
Hopes awaken, tender light,
While winter's grip does astound.

Every flake tells a story spun,
Of sunshine captured, now transformed.
In the silence, whispers run,
Within the chill, dreams are warmed.

Anticipation fills the space,
As dawn approaches, light will rise.
Snowflakes kiss the earth's embrace,
A promise held in winter's guise.

The world shimmers, pristine glow,
Each moment sparks with potential.
In frozen lanes, the heart will know,
Life unfolds, transcendental.

Underneath the ice, a pulse beats,
A rhythm hidden, soft and bold.
Through the cold, destiny greets,
Glimmers flash, stories unfold.

Nature's Palette of Frost and Thought

Brushstrokes of white, a canvas wide,
Nature paints with frosty hands.
Thoughts unravel, dreams abide,
In the quiet of winter's lands.

Each crystal sparkles, a moment caught,
Underneath the churning skies.
In frozen silence, lessons taught,
Life's mysteries in the cold arise.

Colors blend in twilight's art,
Shadows dance where sunlight wanes.
In every hue, the heart plays part,
A symphony of joys and pains.

With every breath, the air feels new,
Transcending sorrow, embracing grace.
In winter's chill, life's essence grew,
Creating warmth in the coldest place.

Awake, the world in silence speaks,
A dialogue between earth and sky.
In nature's palette, solace peaks,
As peace settles with the night.

Subtle Touches of the Cold

Whispers in the frosty air,
Gentle breaths of winter's care.
Each step leaves a crystal trace,
Nature's breath, a soft embrace.

Branches bow with graceful weight,
Silvery shades, a quiet slate.
The world slows, the stillness grows,
Beneath the chill, a beauty flows.

A shiver dances on my skin,
Silent secrets held within.
Moments pause, the heart feels bold,
In subtle touches of the cold.

Frosted Lace on the Mind's Canvas

Glimmers weave through winter's mist,
Each thought a frosted artist's twist.
Patterns spun on memory's thread,
Lace of white where dreams are fed.

Frozen whispers spark delight,
Reflections in the pale moonlight.
Imagination drifts and sways,
In chilly hues, the spirit plays.

A tapestry, serene and bright,
We dance through shadows and through light.
Frosted lace, a tender bond,
On the mind's canvas, dreams respond.

Winter's Gentle Lullaby

Softly falls the evening snow,
A lullaby that starts to flow.
Nature hums a soothing tune,
Beneath the silver, watch the moon.

Whispers curl against the breeze,
The world wraps in a quiet freeze.
Each flake sings a fragile song,
In winter's arms, we all belong.

As trees sway in the twilight glow,
Time stands still, a gentle show.
Embraced by dreams, we softly sigh,
Captured by winter's lullaby.

Remnants of Frost-Kissed Whispers

Morning breaks with tender light,
Frosty whispers take their flight.
Each breath a story, soft and clear,
Remnants left for us to hear.

Nature sings a hushed refrain,
In the chill, there's warmth to gain.
Memories carved on windows bright,
Frost-kissed dreams in purest white.

A moment frozen, yet alive,
Through the stillness, hopes arrive.
Whispers echo, time slips by,
In remnants of frost-kissed sighs.

Dreams Wrapped in White

In a field of snow, silence reigns,
Whispers of winter brush the plains.
Cotton clouds drift, gently they fall,
Hiding soft secrets, enthralling us all.

Footprints lead where shadows play,
In the stillness, dreams drift away.
The moon, a guardian, glows so bright,
Wrapping our hopes in the purest white.

Stars twinkle softly, a celestial creed,
In the heart of the night, they plant a seed.
Each heartbeat echoes, a lullaby sweet,
As we drift further in this snowy retreat.

Branches bend low under snowy weight,
Nature's embrace feels like fate.
In these moments, we find our peace,
In dreams wrapped in white, our worries cease.

As dawn approaches, pastel skies bloom,
The world awakens, chasing the gloom.
Yet still we cherish the night's calming sighs,
For in dreams wrapped in white, our spirit flies.

Melting Ice and Flickering Ideas

Underneath the frost, sparkles gleam,
Ideas flicker like a fleeting dream.
Ice slowly shatters, water flows free,
Creative currents dance, wild and carefree.

Sculptures of winter begin to fade,
Revealing the life that the cold has stayed.
Thoughts cascade like droplets in spring,
Melting ice, the warmth we bring.

Every crack in the surface tells a tale,
Of visions that glimmer and never pale.
In the chaos, inspiration ignites,
As melting ice fuels our daring flights.

Echoes of laughter fill the air,
In this season of change, we find our share.
Ideas burst forth, like blooms in the sun,
Melting ice whispers, our work is begun.

With each thaw, the world feels new,
In the light of creation, dreams burst through.
So gather these moments, embrace each ray,
Where melting ice leads us, we'll boldly stray.

Echoes of the Frozen Mind

In the still of the night, thoughts intertwine,
Frozen reflections in moonlit design.
Echoes linger where silence prevails,
Whispers of secrets in silvery trails.

Thoughts encased like ice in the air,
Fleeting visions float without a care.
In this frozen realm, we seek to explore,
Layers of meaning in the mind's décor.

Time takes shape like snowflakes that fall,
Each one unique, dancing through the hall.
Memories glisten on cold crystal shores,
Echoes remind us of ancient wishes and more.

The mind, a labyrinth, sharp and confined,
Yet in winter's grasp, it starts to unwind.
Each frozen thought, now begins to thaw,
Revealing the beauty in the silent awe.

As the dawn beckons, shadows recede,
The echoes of winter plant the seed.
A journey within, where the soul finds its kind,
Unveiling the layers of the frozen mind.

Winter's Clarity

Amidst the chill, the world stands still,
Clarity blooms from the wintry will.
Each breath crystallizes in the cold air,
Moments sharp as daggers, rare and fair.

Frosted branches frame the bright skies,
In winter's embrace, truth never lies.
Every flake that falls, a story to tell,
In this quiet season, we learn to dwell.

The stillness speaks, a voice so profound,
In the hush of snow, wisdom is found.
Nature reveals what the heart must see,
In winter's clarity, we can just be.

Thoughts float like snowflakes, pure and bright,
Drifting slowly through the long, dark night.
With every dawn, the light starts to creep,
Winter's clarity, a gift we keep.

As daylight stretches and shadows play,
We gather insights from the day.
In nature's mirror, we find our way,
Embracing the truth as we wake and sway.

Luminescent Thoughts of the Frost

In the quiet of the dawn,
Whispers dance on icy air.
Glimmers spark on frosted hues,
Dreams unfurl without a care.

Crystals sparkle on the ground,
Nature's art in cold repose.
Every breath a fleeting mist,
A secret wind, as silence grows.

Thoughts like snowflakes gently swirl,
Each unique in chilly flight.
Moments frozen in their grace,
Time suspends, a pure delight.

Stars above, a shimmering veil,
Softly sewn in dusky skies.
Dusk and dawn in harmony,
Frosted thoughts begin to rise.

In this world of pale and frost,
Beauty finds its tranquil place.
Luminescent, fleeting dreams,
Reflecting winter's soft embrace.

The Quietude of Frozen Fantasies

Softly falls the white cascade,
A world wrapped in stillness deep.
Whispers echo through the trees,
In the night, the shadows creep.

Dreams are woven in the frost,
Trailing trails of icy grace.
Every flake a fleeting thought,
In this calm, we find our space.

Candles flicker, shadows dance,
As the moonlight softly glows.
Frozen whispers of the night,
Guard the tales that winter knows.

Stars align in silken skies,
Painting dreams in silver light.
Time retreats, the coldness hums,
In this quiet, hearts take flight.

Ephemeral, the frozen realm,
Where fantasies are set free.
In the stillness of the night,
Winter's magic calls to me.

An Elegy for Winter's Embrace

Silent falls the snow on earth,
A gentle blanket covers all.
In its hush, a world reborn,
Winter's grace, a quiet call.

Frigid air, the breath of night,
Each inhale stirs unseen dreams.
Echoes of the past resound,
In the calm, a quiet stream.

Memories of summer's glow,
Seep into the snow's embrace.
Lost in time, we wander slow,
In this chill, our hearts find space.

Yet within the cold, there's warmth,
A fire kindled deep within.
As we clutch these fleeting days,
Let the winter's song begin.

Elegies for times gone past,
Each flake tells a story cold.
As we gather 'round the hearth,
Winter's tales will now unfold.

Rhythms of the Ice-Wrapped Soul

Beneath the weight of winter's quilt,
The earth pulses with quiet might.
In the hush, a subtle beat,
Echoes of the stars at night.

Icicles hang like crystal chimes,
Their beauty sharp against the chill.
Nature hums a frosty tune,
As rhythm flows from vale to hill.

Every breath a fleeting note,
As whispers travel through the air.
In this symphony of frost,
We find solace everywhere.

The night drapes her velvet cloak,
Softly cradling dreams untold.
In the silence, we can hear,
The stories of the brave and bold.

Life continues, ebb and flow,
Wrapped in ice, yet warm inside.
The rhythm of the frozen world,
Keeps our hearts in soft abide.

The Breath of Winter's Chill

Whispers drift through frosty air,
A silence wrapped in slumber's care.
Each breath a ghost, a sigh released,\nWinter's hold, a quiet feast.

Icicles hanging from the trees,
Nature's art with graceful ease.
The world adorned in purest white,
A tranquil spell, a peaceful night.

Footsteps crunch on frozen ground,
A symphony of silence found.
In icy realms, the heart beats slow,
Embracing chill, a gentle flow.

Stars aglow in velvet skies,
The breath of winter softly sighs.
Underneath the moonlit glow,
Dreams of warmth begin to grow.

Life's embers fade, yet still remain,
In winter's grip, a curious pain.
For in the cold, we find our way,
A path of light in shades of gray.

Crystal Shards of Thought

Fragments glinting in the mind,
Ideas dance, elusive, blind.
Shards of dreams, reflections bright,
Fleeting visions in the night.

Each thought a prism, bright and clear,
Piercing through the veil of fear.
In the quiet, they collide,
Crafting worlds we cannot hide.

Minds a canvas, blank and wide,
Colors merge, like waves, they ride.
Painted moments, bright and bold,
Stories waiting to be told.

In the stillness, whispers rise,
Thoughts as vivid as the skies.
Cascading light, a silent song,
Guiding us where we belong.

Glimmers fade, yet still they stay,
Tracing paths in shades of gray.
With each breath, new shards are formed,
In crystal clarity, we're warmed.

Shimmering Mists of Clarity

Veils of fog embrace the dawn,
What is lost begins to yawn.
In the haze, truth starts to show,
Glimmers of what we ought to know.

Softly floating, dreams take flight,
Mists revealing hidden light.
In the tender morning air,
Clarity breaks the silent glare.

Thoughts like ripples, gentle waves,
Flowing through the heart like braves.
Each step taken, new paths drawn,
With shimmering mists, we move on.

Secrets hidden, soft and bright,
In the fog, they find their light.
Like whispers in a quiet room,
Clarity dispels the gloom.

As the day begins to rise,
Mists dissolve, unveil the skies.
With each dawn, possibilities,
Shimmering paths, set minds at ease.

Thoughts like Snowflakes

Each thought a flake, unique and rare,
Dancing softly through the air.
Delicate whispers, gentle grace,
Carving patterns, leaving trace.

Falling gently to the ground,
In their landing, peace is found.
Whirling, spiraling, they descend,
Stories spun that never end.

In the stillness, wonder grows,
Snowflakes whisper, no one knows.
Captured moments, brief and sweet,
Laced with magic, bittersweet.

So let them fall, let them play,
In the silence, thoughts convey.
Each flake a spark, a fleeting chance,
Creating worlds in quiet dance.

As they melt, new thoughts will bloom,
In the heart, they find their room.
Thoughts like snowflakes, soft and bright,
Crafting warmth in winter's light.

Glimmering Dreams of White

In the hush of a gentle night,
Snowflakes fall, a soft delight.
Blankets white upon the ground,
Whispers of dreams that wrap around.

Stars above start to gleam,
Casting light on the frosty theme.
Footprints traced, a silent song,
In glimmering dreams, we belong.

Trees adorned with crystal lace,
Nature's beauty, a tranquil space.
Frosty breath hangs in the air,
Moments captured, rare and fair.

In the stillness, hearts ignite,
Chasing shadows, pure and bright.
Winds of winter softly play,
Guiding dreams that drift away.

Underneath the moon's soft glow,
Magic found in the falling snow.
Glimmering dreams, forever bliss,
In each flake, a lover's kiss.

Pondering in the Cold

Wind whispers secrets through the trees,
In the chill, I find my peace.
Thoughts meander like the snow,
Pondering where the shadows go.

Frozen lakes keep silent grace,
Mirroring the winter's face.
Footsteps crunching on the ground,
Echoes of the calm profound.

Underneath the grayish skies,
Hope still twinkles in our eyes.
With each breath, a cloud appears,
A fleeting moment, held for years.

Branches heavy with the weight,
Nature's heart begins to wait.
Time stands still in the winter's mold,
As I ponder in the cold.

Every flake a story told,
Whispers carried, brave and bold.
In this frost, I find my way,
Pondering life on a winter's day.

Frigid Reflections

In the mirror of the frozen sea,
I see the world, so endlessly.
Clouds drift by, shadows merge,
In frigid reflections, thoughts converge.

Ice cascades, a brilliant sight,
Painting whispers deep of night.
Silent echoes, softly cast,
Each moment cherished, held steadfast.

The chill creeps in, a tender touch,
Yet wrapped in warmth, it means so much.
Glistening paths that lead us on,
Frigid reflections at the dawn.

Nature's peace cloaked in white,
Fragments of day, fading light.
Each breath of frost, a chance to grow,
In this silence, wisdom flows.

Through the cold, my heart is bold,
Wandering through tales untold.
In frigid reflections, I find grace,
A quiet moment, a sacred space.

Winter's Serene Silence

Softly drapes the snow at night,
Hushed the world, a pure delight.
Winter's breath, a gentle sigh,
In the silence, spirits fly.

Pine trees stand in quiet mode,
Wearing white, a noble code.
Every flake that falls from grace,
Paints a picture, time and space.

In the calm, the heart can hear,
Stories whispered, crystal clear.
Nature pauses, love defined,
In winter's silence, peace we find.

Stars gaze down with twinkling eyes,
Illuminating endless skies.
A blanket wraps the world so tight,
In winter's arms, all feels right.

Let the season's magic glow,
In this tranquil, frosty show.
Winter's serene silence sings,
In the heart, it gently clings.

Thoughts Adrift in Frost

Thoughts drift like leaves in the cold,
Whispering secrets, stories untold.
Beneath the ice, memories lie,
Waiting for spring to reach for the sky.

Frost paints the world in silvery hues,
Quietly cloaking the morning blues.
Each breath clouds in the chilly air,
Dreams linger softly, with whispered care.

Night falls early, shadows play,
Memories flicker, then fade away.
Time is frozen, moments decay,
In the stillness, I find my way.

Footsteps crunch on the icy ground,
Echos of thoughts that swirl around.
Lost in the maze of winter's breath,
Searching for warmth amidst the death.

Yet in the frost, hope can arise,
Beneath the stillness, a spark that flies.
Ideas awaken, breaking the freeze,
In the heart of cold, there's always ease.

Mindscapes of Snow

Snowflakes dance in the gentle breeze,
Blanketing earth with silent ease.
Thoughts wander like flurries on high,
Painting the canvas of a gray sky.

In the hush, whispers softly roam,
Seeking a place they can call home.
Ideas build like drifts on the ground,
In this white world, clarity is found.

Each crystal sparkles, a fleeting glance,
A moment of beauty, a fleeting chance.
Minds awaken in the soft glow,
Of winter's magic, an ethereal show.

Guided by stars that twinkle bright,
Illuminating paths in the night.
Dreams intertwine with the cold air,
Unraveling mysteries, without a care.

As the snow falls, tranquility flows,
A gentle reminder of the world's woes.
Yet beneath, the mind's fire burns slow,
In the heart of the snow, creativity grows.

Hibernating Ideas

Beneath the frost, ideas sleep,
Wrapped in silence, secrets to keep.
Dreams lie dormant, waiting their time,
In the quiet layers of winter's rhyme.

Thoughts huddle close, nestled warm,
In the calm of the cold, they form.
Seeds of brilliance, hidden from sight,
Biding their moment to spring into light.

Winter whispers, a lullaby sweet,
Encouraging rest, allowing retreat.
Minds take shelter from chaos and noise,
Finding solace in simplicity's joys.

Though the world may seem still and gray,
Creativity lingers, ready to sway.
With each thaw, new visions ignite,
From the heart of winter, takes flight.

In this season of quiet decay,
Hibernating thoughts will find their way.
Awakening gently, with the sun's rise,
Renewed and vibrant, a sparkling surprise.

The Frosty Labyrinth of Thought

Lost in the maze of frosty air,
Wandering through the chill's silent lair.
Each corner turned reveals a new view,
Reflections shimmering, deep and true.

A labyrinth formed by winter's hand,
Where icy pathways lead to distant lands.
Thoughts meander like streams in frost,
Seeking the warmth of what was lost.

Fingers trace patterns in the snow,
Mapping the journey of what we know.
In the frozen stillness, clarity stirs,
As the wind carries unsaid words.

Shadows stretch under the pale moon,
A haunting melody, a distant tune.
In the frost's embrace, ideas collide,
Merging and shifting, with nowhere to hide.

Yet amidst the cold, sparks begin to glow,
Fired by passion, chased by the flow.
Through the frosty maze, they find their light,
Illuminating paths, breaking the night.

Layers of Ice and Insight

Beneath the frost, a story waits,
Whispers of time in frozen states.
A surface shimmering, cold and clear,
Echoes of thoughts we hold so dear.

Cracks reveal what lies below,
Hidden truths in the icy glow.
With each fracture, new paths bend,
A journey begun that has no end.

The stillness sings, a haunting call,
In this silence, we stand tall.
Complexity wrapped in a chill,
Yet in the void, we find our will.

Beneath the ice, seeds of change lie,
Waiting for warmth, a chance to fly.
Layers unfold with every dawn,
In the frost, we are reborn.

In winter's grasp, we seek to know,
The beauty amidst the biting snow.
With each layer, insights unfold,
In the silence, stories told.

Winter's Gentle Muse

Snowflakes dance in tranquil air,
Painting landscapes, bright and rare.
Each flake a whisper, soft as dream,
Crafting visions, a serene theme.

Through crystal branches, shadows play,
In winter's arms, the world turns gray.
Yet within that muted light,
Dreams awaken, taking flight.

The quiet hum of nature's pause,
A sacred time without a cause.
Each breath reveals a hidden grace,
In winter's chill, we find our place.

Upon the hills, the blankets lie,
Glistening jewels under the sky.
The silence speaks, it's profound,
In this stillness, we are found.

Fragments of warmth, memories cling,
To the heart as the cold winds sing.
In the biting air, muse ignites,
Creating art in frosty nights.

In the Quiet of Winter

Snow envelops the world tight,
Blanketing all in purest white.
Footsteps softened, whispers fade,
In winter's hush, a serenade.

Branches bow with a silken load,
Each flake a point on a quiet road.
The crystal sparkles, a gentle gleam,
Amidst the calm, we dare to dream.

Fires crackle, warmth from within,
As outside whispers the cool wind's hymn.
In flickers of light, stories brew,
Of seasons past and futures new.

In the stillness, thoughts intertwine,
Reflecting on life, a sacred sign.
The world pauses, a moment to be,
In the quiet, we find clarity.

Nature rests, preparing to wake,
In winter's arms, we mend and remake.
Though the chill wraps tight around,
In this solitude, hope is found.

Thoughts Under a White Mantle

A blanket of snow on the earth spills,
Draping the grounds with serene chills.
Leaves have fallen, yet stories remain,
Wrapped in white, a soft refrain.

Thoughts drift softly like flakes in the air,
Carried by winds that whisper and care.
In this quiet embrace, reflections grow,
Under the white, we learn to let go.

Winter's breath weaves through the trees,
Lingering scents on a crisp, cool breeze.
Moments of pause, the heartbeats sync,
In the silence, we start to think.

Under the mantle, life slows down,
Layers of beauty in the frosty town.
In each flake, a memory lies,
A gentle reminder as the past flies.

The world transformed, a canvas bright,
In the glow of dawn's gentle light.
Though winter holds us, spring draws near,
Under its watch, we conquer fear.

Whispers of Winter's Embrace

Hushed winds sing of snowflakes,
Blanketing the world in white,
Trees wear coats of crystal lace,
As day gives way to night.

Moonlight dances on the frost,
Casting shadows soft and pale,
In this quiet, nothing's lost,
Winter weaves its tranquil tale.

Each breath rises into the air,
A fleeting sigh, a gentle pause,
Life slows down; we take more care,
To cherish nature's quiet cause.

Footsteps crunch on icy ground,
Echoes carry through the trees,
In solitude, a peace is found,
As whispers float upon the breeze.

Embrace the chill; feel the grace,
In winter's arms, we'll find our place.

Frosted Reveries

Morning light breaks soft and sweet,
Warming shadows, night retreats,
With frost adorning every frame,
Nature whispers, never tamed.

The garden sleeps beneath a shroud,
Each petal glistens, proud and loud,
A world transformed in silver hue,
Awakening dreams, fresh and new.

Birds return with melodies clear,
Serenading winter's frontier,
Bright notes soar through crisp, cold air,
Frosted reveries everywhere.

Coffee brews, the fires burn,
In cozy corners, hearts will yearn,
For warmth in touch, and stories shared,
As winter lingers, love is bared.

Embrace the chill, let visions spark,
In frosted dreams, ignite the dark.

Shivering Dreams

In quiet nights where shadows creep,
Snowflakes tumble, hush the deep,
While whispers echo in the outer,
Fires crackle, cradling our chatter.

Beneath blankets, dreams take flight,
Frosted panes; a delicate sight,
We dance in realms of winter's lore,
Tailored by holds of evermore.

Restless hearts weave through the cold,
Longing for moments, bright and bold,
Each shiver tells a tale anew,
Of love's warmth, forever true.

In the glow of the ember's light,
We share secrets, take delight,
Awakening visions, soft and grand,
Together we stand, hand in hand.

Through shivering dreams we find our way,
In winter's heart, we choose to stay.

Crystal Clarity

Morning reveals a world anew,
Wrapped in frost, the earth feels true,
Sunlight strikes like shards of glass,
As time meanders, none can pass.

Each flake tells a story bright,
Of whispered joys in cold delight,
Nature's canvas, clear and bright,
Holds secrets in the soft twilight.

Through branches bare, the crystal sighs,
Winter breathes beneath the skies,
In silence, every truth is found,
Life distilled in beauty abound.

Reflections dance on icy streams,
Captured softly are our dreams,
In moments frozen, perfectly spun,
We find the clarity of the sun.

Embrace the still; let visions grow,
In winter's heart, love's warmth we know.

Winter's Veil of Reflection

The world is shrouded in white,
Soft whispers in the night air.
Frosty branches reaching high,
Time stops in the frosted glare.

Thoughts drift like snowflakes fall,
Each one unique, spinning slow.
Mirrors of memory call,
In stillness, truths we know.

Under the weight of the chill,
Nature pauses, breath is held.
Silent beauty, quiet thrill,
Wondrous secrets are compelled.

Footsteps crunch on icy ground,
Echoes linger in the stream.
Lost in the magic found,
Awake from a timeless dream.

Winter's breath, a gentle sigh,
Reflects the warmth of our hearts.
As days pass, we draw nigh,
In peace, the winter imparts.

Chilled Epiphany

Beneath the frostbitten skies,
A sudden clarity takes flight.
Thoughts crystallize, then arise,
In the chill of the dawning light.

Frozen moments, sharp and clear,
Truth cuts through the winter haze.
Epiphanies whisper near,
Guiding us through the cold maze.

Snow blankets the sleeping earth,
Cradling dreams in its embrace.
In the silence, there's rebirth,
A soft touch on time's still face.

Fires crackle with warm glow,
Hearts ignite with deep desire.
In the cold, our spirits grow,
Fueling the inner fire.

As twilight paints the world gray,
A chill wraps around my soul.
In the quiet, thoughts at play,
Chilled epiphanies make us whole.

Fragments of Ice

Shards glisten under the moon,
Each a story once untold.
In the stillness of the noon,
Nature's treasures, bright and bold.

Crystalline structures arise,
Fragments scattered, glimmering bright.
Beauty captured in surprise,
Twinkling softly in the night.

As the sun begins to rise,
Melting moments now unfold.
Heartfelt whispers, silent sighs,
Warmth drapes over, tender, bold.

In the dance of fleeting light,
I find solace in the chill.
Each fragment holds a delight,
Time lingers, yet stands still.

Winter's canvas, vast and wide,
Crafted by nature's own design.
In its folds, the world can bide,
Fragments of ice, pure and divine.

Silent Mornings in White

A hush blankets the crisp ground,
Gentle flakes drift from the skies.
In this stillness, peace is found,
Winter's magic, pure surprise.

Clouds bathe the earth in calm,
Softly whispering the breeze.
Nature's breath is like a balm,
Wrapped in warmth, it aims to please.

Silent mornings, pure and bright,
As shadows dance on the snow.
With every dawn, a new light,
Promises of warmth that grow.

Footsteps trace the patterns clear,
Painting paths upon the white.
In these moments, calm and near,
Silent hearts take joyful flight.

With each sunrise, hope returns,
Embraced in the winter's glow.
In our hearts, the flame still burns,
Silent mornings set us free.

Flakes of Insight

Snowflakes fall softly down,
Each one a unique crown.
In silence, wisdom unfolds,
Stories of wonders untold.

Naked branches touch the sky,
Nature's breath is a sigh.
In the stillness, we find peace,
Moments of joy that never cease.

Footprints mark the crystal white,
Guided by the soft moonlight.
In every step, a new thought,
Life's lessons gently caught.

Glimmers of truth melt away,
Like the ice that won't stay.
In reflection, we embrace,
The beauty of life's grace.

Flakes of insight drift and sway,
In the heart's quiet play.
As winter claims the day bright,
We find warmth in the light.

Meditations on a Winter's Day

Morning light begins to glow,
Revealing worlds beneath the snow.
Thoughts like whispers in the breeze,
Rustle gently in the trees.

Breath of winter, crisp and cool,
Nature's silence, a sacred rule.
In the stillness, we reflect,
Moments of time to connect.

The heart beats a steady rhyme,
In the solitude of time.
The world outside seems far away,
In our minds, we softly play.

Candles flicker, shadows dance,
In the quiet, we take a chance.
To seek the light within our souls,
Finding peace, making us whole.

Snowflakes carry dreams anew,
Glistening in morning dew.
Embrace the whispers, let them guide,
In winter's arms, we abide.

Whispers of Frosted Dreams

In the hush of frosted night,
Dreams take flight, soft and light.
Stars twinkle like distant thoughts,
In the silence, wisdom's sought.

Winter's breath kisses the ground,
In its charm, magic is found.
Each flake a message from the sky,
Whispers of dreams that never die.

Moonlight glimmers on the snow,
Guiding hearts where they should go.
In the chill, there's warmth of grace,
In every frozen, sacred space.

Time stands still, a gentle pause,
In nature's arms, we find the cause.
Reflections dance in icy streams,
Telling tales of frosted dreams.

Footsteps silent, paths untraced,
In this moment, we find our place.
Let the whispers guide our way,
Through the beauty of the day.

Chilled Echoes of Serenity

Frozen echoes in the air,
A stillness beyond compare.
Nature's breath, a gentle sigh,
Whispers soft as clouds drift by.

Each moment wrapped in crystal chill,
Calming hearts, the world stands still.
In the hush, we find our peace,
As time itself seems to cease.

Footprints lead to dreams unspun,
Each one tells of battles won.
In the quiet, strength is found,
Chilled echoes all around.

Let the frost adorn our hearts,
In this stillness, love imparts.
Life's symphony plays soft and low,
In winter's arms, we learn to grow.

Serenity in every breath,
A reminder of love, not death.
Through chilled echoes, souls align,
In winter's grace, we are divine.

Whispered Hopes in a Blizzard

Snowflakes dance in swirling light,
Caught within a winter's flight.
Words like whispers fill the air,
Hopes and dreams beyond compare.

Through the storm, a vision gleams,
Frosted paths and silver beams.
In the silence, heartbeats sound,
Life's intentions all around.

Underneath the heavy skies,
Lies a truth that never dies.
With each flake that gently falls,
Echoes of our long-lost calls.

Blinding white both near and far,
Guides us like a distant star.
In the chaos, find the calm,
Hope is held like winter's balm.

As the blizzard starts to fade,
New beginnings will be made.
In the quiet, dreams take flight,
Whispered hopes in endless night.

Glacial Thoughts that Drift and Flow

Thoughts like rivers, cold and pure,
Flow through landscapes, soft allure.
Silence wraps the frozen ground,
In the stillness, truths are found.

Every moment, crisp and clear,
Whispers echo, drawing near.
Memories like ice can freeze,
In the heart, a gentle breeze.

Drifting gently, not in haste,
Nature's beauty, sweetly chaste.
Glacial thoughts, both wise and bold,
Stories waiting to be told.

Winding paths of icy streams,
Carry wishes, hold our dreams.
In their flow, we find our way,
Glacial thoughts that softly sway.

As the world begins to thaw,
New reflections, deeper awe.
Embrace the journey, let it show,
Glacial thoughts that drift and flow.

The Solemn Beauty of Winter's Mind

Winter's breath, both chill and bright,
Whispers secrets cloaked in white.
Trees stand tall, in still repose,
Guardians of the dreams that froze.

Shadows stretch as daylight wanes,
In the quiet, beauty reigns.
Frosted leaves and icy trails,
Tell the tales of winter gales.

Time moves slowly, yet it's fast,
Moments frozen, shadows cast.
In the silence, wisdom lies,
Winter's mind beneath the skies.

Snowflakes gather, soft embrace,
Nature's canvas, tranquil grace.
Reflections dance on crystal streams,
In the dark, we weave our dreams.

In solemn beauty, we find peace,
As the world begins to cease.
In the depths of winter's mind,
Endless wonders we will find.

Sweet Shadows of the Arctic Night

In the depths where silence dwells,
Sweet shadows spin their whispered spells.
Moonlight glimmers on the snow,
In the dark, our thoughts will grow.

Stars like diamonds dot the sky,
In their glow, the dreams can fly.
Shadows dance on frozen streams,
Carved in time, the night's soft themes.

Whispers float on icy breeze,
Carrying our heartfelt pleas.
In the chill, a warmth ignites,
Sweet shadows of the Arctic nights.

Winds that sing a lullaby,
Cradle us as we sigh.
Every heartbeat in the deep,
Tales of winter, secrets keep.

Through the silence, spirits rise,
In the dark, a million sighs.
Underneath the endless heights,
Sweet shadows of the Arctic nights.

Icy Reveries

In the hush of winter's breath,
Dreams float in crystal air,
Whispers of a cold caress,
Captured moments, rich and rare.

Moonlight drapes the frozen ground,
Shadows dance on glistening white,
A world where silence wears a crown,
Every heartbeat laced with light.

Snowflakes twirl like distant stars,
Falling softly from the sky,
Nature's beauty, pure and far,
Invites our spirits to comply.

Through the woods, the footsteps fade,
Leaving echoes of the night,
Frosted branches serenade,
Underneath the silver light.

A fleeting waltz of chilly dreams,
In solitude, we find our place,
As winter's spell quietly redeems,
The heart's longing for grace.

Frosty Epilogues

Beneath the veil of icy air,
Stories linger, faint and shy,
Memory's breath, a frosty layer,
Woven in the night's soft sigh.

Frozen echoes roam the land,
Each footfall whispers tales untold,
Nature's canvas, stark and grand,
A tapestry of blue and gold.

In every crystal, life resides,
Dancing lightly on the breeze,
While time in frigid beauty hides,
Moments held like gentle freeze.

Branches bow in quiet peace,
Beneath the heavy blanket's hold,
Each silence offers sweet release,
As warmth within the heart unfolds.

A midnight melody takes wing,
Softly whispering to the soul,
Frosty tales that winter brings,
With every sigh, we become whole.

The Stillness in the Snow

A quiet hush, a world asleep,
Beneath the blanket, pure and white,
In this moment, secrets keep,
The soft embrace of winter night.

Footprints trace a fragile path,
Stories trapped in frozen time,
Nature's peace, a gentle bath,
In every drift, a whispered rhyme.

Stars above, like diamonds, gleam,
Casting light on slumbering trees,
Dreams unfurl like a silent dream,
Cradled in the frigid breeze.

As shadows weave and silence reigns,
The heart finds solace in the still,
While frosty air like silver chains,
Wraps the world with tranquil thrill.

In this stillness, life renews,
Pausing for a moment's grace,
The snowy veil, a soft muse,
Invites our souls to slow their pace.

Chilling Contemplations

In winter's grasp, reflections grow,
Thoughts drift on the frosty streams,
Each chill a nudge to linger slow,
As night unveils our hidden dreams.

The biting air ignites the mind,
A quiet call to dwell within,
In this cold space, truth we find,
Where shadows dance, and fears grow thin.

Frosty breath, a song of peace,
Beneath the stars, we ponder long,
In silence, heartaches find release,
A soothing balm, a gentle song.

As flakes descend from heavy skies,
Each one a wish, a whispered prayer,
In their descent, the spirit flies,
Finding warmth in winter's glare.

So let us pause, breathe in the cold,
Embrace each moment, fierce and bright,
Through chilling thoughts, our truths unfold,
Guided by the moon's soft light.

Crystalline Thoughts on a Cold Breeze

In the stillness of dawn's light,
Whispers dance on frosty air,
Each thought glimmers like glass,
Captured moments everywhere.

Softly twirling in the chill,
Dreams unfold like petals bright,
Tender feelings brush my soul,
Held in hues of pure delight.

A crystal garden springs alive,
With each breath, the beauty grows,
Thoughts like snowflakes gently fall,
In a world that softly glows.

Heartbeats echo, crisp and clear,
As the cold weaves through the pines,
In the hush, a promise stirs,
Alive in rhythm, love aligns.

Into the vast, I send my hopes,
Carried forth on winter's sigh,
Crystalline whispers in the air,
Marking dreams that dare to fly.

Shadows of Ice in Quiet Corners

In corners where the light won't reach,
Shadows linger, cold and shy,
Quiet tales of winter's heart,
Whisper secrets as they sigh.

Frosted panes and muffled sounds,
Icicles hang like frozen tears,
In silence, they collect the years,
Beneath the weight of hopes and fears.

Yet in the dark, a spark might glow,
Hidden warmth beneath the freeze,
Love's soft echo breaks the night,
As shadows dance with gentle ease.

Each breath visible in the frost,
A fleeting moment comes and goes,
Through the ice, a fracture forms,
New possibilities arise as the winter flows.

In quiet corners, magic stirs,
Beneath the frozen, hardened crust,
Emerging light reveals the truth,
In darkest depths, we find our trust.

Frost's Embrace on Vulnerable Hearts

Beneath the chill of winter skies,
Vulnerable hearts beat slow,
Wrapped in frost's delicate arms,
In a dance where feelings flow.

Thin ice forms on fragile dreams,
Cracking softly with each sigh,
Yet beneath the frozen surface,
Warmth of love dares to fly.

In every flake that gently falls,
A promise rests, pure and bright,
For through the gloom, a spark ignites,
Mending wounds in shadows light.

The quiet night holds tender truths,
As stars reflect in icy pools,
Hearts entwined in winter's grasp,
Finding warmth where silence rules.

With every step, we tread the path,
Trusting the frost, embracing change,
In the heart of winter's breath,
Lives the love we rearrange.

Chasing the Winter's Shadow

In the fading light of day,
Winter whispers hints of night,
Shadows long, they stretch and yawn,
Dancing on the edge of sight.

Footsteps soft on powdered ground,
Chasing echoes, memories clear,
Hidden paths where silence reigns,
Drawn by winter's quiet cheer.

Each corner holds a story told,
Through frostbitten trees and skies,
In the hush, a call to dream,
Where every shadow gently lies.

Starlit skies, a blanket warm,
Embrace the chill, let spirits soar,
In the chase, we find our peace,
As winter hums its ancient score.

Through the frost, our heartbeats blend,
Chasing shadows, we unite,
In the dance of winter's grace,
Together, we ignite the night.

Murmurs of a Winter Spirit

Whispers dance upon the frost,
Breezes weave a tale of loss.
Silent echoes fill the air,
Winter's breath, a whispered prayer.

Moonlight glimmers on the snow,
Casting shadows, soft and low.
Footprints fade where dreams have tread,
Guiding spirits of the dead.

Branches bow with crystal weight,
Nature's crown, a fragile state.
Hushed tones linger in the night,
Carried forth by pale moonlight.

Fires crackle, warmth inside,
Hearts embrace the cold with pride.
Murmurs rise like smoke in air,
Winter's song is everywhere.

In the stillness, peace unfolds,
Stories new and those retold.
Murmurs of a spirit's grace,
In the winter's warm embrace.

Dreams Beneath the Icicles

Icicles hang like frozen tears,
Mirrors of our ancient fears.
Underneath, the whispers sigh,
Where the dreams of winter lie.

Starlit skies, a velvet sheet,
Covering the world in sweet.
Beneath the chill, a fire glows,
Warmth of hope that gently flows.

Shadows flicker, soft and wise,
As the night begins to rise.
Delicate as frost that forms,
Dreams awaken in the storms.

Frosty breath, the silence shatters,
In the night, our spirit scatters.
Rays of dawn break through the cold,
Turning dreams to tales untold.

Awake beneath the gleaming ice,
Finding solace, finding light.
In the quiet, we will find,
Dreams beneath, forever blind.

Fragments of Glacial Reverie

Crystal shards of memory gleam,
Fragments of an endless dream.
Frozen lakes and silent nights,
Holding on to winter's sights.

Whispers of the ancient trees,
Dancing lightly on the breeze.
Frigid air, a calming balm,
Nature's touch, forever calm.

Reflections in the icy blue,
Captured moments, pure and true.
Time stands still in winter's reign,
Glacial hearts know hush and pain.

Voices hush in moon's embrace,
Embers glow with every trace.
Fragments lost to time, but clear,
Memories that we hold dear.

In the calm, the thoughts collide,
In glacial dreams, we confide.
All the moments, softly spun,
Fragments whisper, we are one.

Frostbitten Flurries of Emotion

Snowflakes kiss the window pane,
With each fall, a soft refrain.
Frostbitten flurries twirl and play,
Capturing the heart's ballet.

Chilled breaths curl into the night,
Spirits glowing, burning bright.
Emotions drift like winter's breath,
Life and love, a dance with death.

In the stillness, feelings rise,
Underneath the starry skies.
Crisp and clear, a heartfelt ache,
Frosty dreams we dare to make.

Every flurry, a story spun,
Emotions woven, never done.
Together we embrace the cold,
Frostbitten tales of love retold.

As the night begins to fade,
Memories linger, unafraid.
Frostbitten flurries, soft and light,
Guide our hearts through winter's night.

Serene Landscapes of Thoughts

In a meadow where silence sings,
Gentle breezes brush the seams.
Thoughts like petals float and twirl,
Amidst the quiet, dreams unfurl.

Mountains cradle fading light,
Colors blend in soft twilight.
Each whispering leaf, a word unsaid,
In nature's arms, my heart is led.

A river's flow, a timeless tale,
Guiding souls where shadows pale.
Reflections dance on water's face,
Drawn to peace in this sacred space.

Stars emerge in velvet skies,
Awakening the slumbering sighs.
Each twinkle tells of journeys grand,
Mapping dreams across the land.

Beneath the arching boughs I sit,
In this haven, I gladly commit.
To treasure moments, serene and clear,
In the landscape of thoughts, I revere.

The Chill of Ephemeral Insights

In winter's grasp, a thought takes flight,
A fleeting mind wrapped in white.
Cold breezes carry tales so bright,
Yet vanish like stars in the night.

Each crystal flake, a moment's truth,
A wisdom gained in fleeting youth.
Beneath the frost, ideas hide,
Awaiting warmth to turn the tide.

The barren trees, stark yet wise,
Hold secrets bound to winter skies.
In silence, thoughts begin to form,
Against the chill, a quiet storm.

A breath held close, the world in pause,
Insight whispers, for one good cause.
To seek the warmth in everything,
Even in seasons that coldly cling.

When spring arrives, renewed and bold,
These whispered insights will unfold.
Like budding blooms beneath the freeze,
Life's lessons come with gentle ease.

Frosted Vistas of Contemplation

A landscape draped in icy lace,
Holds the beauty of a dream's embrace.
In the stillness, thoughts snowball,
Each flake a whisper, soft and small.

Mountains rise with snowy crowns,
Guarding secrets beneath their gowns.
Echoes linger, sharp and clear,
In the frosted breath, waiting near.

Sunlight kisses the snowy peak,
Warming hearts, where silence speaks.
Each glance unveils a hidden tale,
A truth that travels like the gale.

The path I walk, a world refined,
Unfolds the treasure of the mind.
As frost retreats and warmth takes hold,
I gather thoughts like seeds to fold.

In every chill, a chance to grow,
In frozen fields, new dreams will flow.
When springtime calls with gentle hand,
The vistas bloom across the land.

Whispers Beneath the Ice

Beneath the surface, silence lays,
In crystalline, encased delays.
Echoes linger in the night,
Undercurrents of hidden light.

Each layer holds a quiet plea,
Voices of what used to be.
Frosted stories, all concealed,
Awaiting warmth to be revealed.

The world above, a fractured sky,
Mountains breathe and rivers sigh.
In tender moments, thoughts arise,
Wrapped in winter's soft disguise.

With every thaw, secrets spill,
A chorus rising, strong and still.
The dance of ice, a fleeting grace,
Invites reflection in this place.

So listen close to nature's hum,
The whispers call, they softly come.
In frozen depths, wisdom lies
Awaiting spring to materialize.

Nature's Whisper in the Winter's Grip

Frosted branches sway and bend,
In silence, whispers start to blend.
A shiver crawls in crisp, cool air,
Nature's breath, both soft and rare.

The world beneath a blanket lies,
Underneath the grayish skies.
Footprints mark the trail we take,
Each step a gentle winter ache.

Hushed are all the lively sounds,
As calm stretches through frosty grounds.
In stillness, nature weaves her spell,
In winter's grip, all is well.

Glittering flakes fall from above,
A testament of silent love.
Each flake a story, soft and bright,
Guided by the moon's pale light.

So let us pause, in awe and cheer,
To celebrate this time so dear.
In winter's grasp, our hearts take flight,
Embracing whispers in the night.

Chilled Sentiments in Crystal Clarity

Frozen morning, clear and bright,
Sparkling crystals catch the light.
Emotions linger in the air,
Chilled sentiments, tender and rare.

Pine trees glisten, cloaked in frost,
In nature's grasp, we find what's lost.
Each breath a fog, a fleeting sight,
Crystal clarity, pure delight.

Echoes of laughter fill the space,
As winter weaves her frosty lace.
Hand in hand, we wander slow,
Through pathways where cold breezes blow.

The world transformed, a stunning scene,
Where heartbeats pulse in shades of green.
These chilly moments, deep and true,
Forever marked, just me and you.

In every flake, a wish we stake,
In crystal clarity, new dreams wake.
In the cold, our spirits soar,
Finding warmth forevermore.

A Symphony of Icicles and Silence

Icicles hang from rooftops high,
A symphony beneath the sky.
Each droplet's fall, a gentle sound,
In silent harmony, we're bound.

The world adorned in winter's grace,
Nature's canvas, a frozen space.
With every note, the silence swells,
In tranquil peace, the heart compels.

Shadows dance on crisp white sheets,
As winter's breath in silence meets.
A melody that's soft and low,
In the quiet, feelings grow.

The sun dips low, a golden hue,
Painting landscapes, fresh and new.
In twilight's glow, the chill remains,
A symphony that gently reigns.

So let us listen, hearts attuned,
To nature's song, both sweet and pruned.
In icicles and silence found,
A symphony of peace profound.

Echoes of Muffled Moments

In twilight's hush, the evening glows,
Echoing whispers in the snows.
Muffled moments drift away,
As daylight fades to night's soft sway.

Footsteps muted on the ground,
A world transformed without a sound.
In winter's arms, we seek to find,
Echoes of love, entwined, designed.

Stars appear like silver pinpoints,
In a sky where silence anoints.
Each glance exchanged, a fleeting touch,
In winter night, it means so much.

The air is thick with dreams and sighs,
While time meanders and softly flies.
With every heartbeat, we embrace,
Muffled moments, a sacred space.

So as we walk this path of light,
Let echoes guide us through the night.
For in the silence, we will find,
Muffled moments, intertwined.

Ethereal Breezes of Solitude

In twilight's grace, whispers flow,
Glimmering dreams that ebb and glow.
Softly they dance, in silence wide,
Embracing the night, where shadows hide.

Breezes trace paths, unseen, untamed,
Carrying secrets, unspoken, unnamed.
Through the stillness, a heart takes flight,
Chasing the stars, elusive light.

Moonlit echoes call out the past,
Moments of joy, fleeting, yet vast.
In solitude found, a calm like none,
Where the soul is cradled, and time is spun.

Nature's breath, a gentle sigh,
Whispers of peace that never die.
In this realm, lost sense unbinds,
Ethereal breezes, where solace finds.

Here in the stillness, I take my stand,
Heart open wide, like grains of sand.
Ethereal breezes coax me to see,
The beauty within, serene and free.

Images Forged in Frost

In winter's grasp, the world ignites,
Images formed on cold, clear nights.
Frosty fingers paint the glass,
Translucent dreams that shimmer and pass.

Each crystal blooms, a fleeting grace,
Nature's canvas, a delicate lace.
Glistening light in the pale dawn's rise,
Mirrored beauty beneath frozen skies.

Shadows linger where silence walks,
Whispers of warmth in the stillness talks.
Pictures unfold in each icy breath,
Life's fragile essence, a dance with death.

Beneath the chill, a heartbeat thrums,
Echoes of life as winter succumbs.
In every flake, a story spun,
Images held, when the day is done.

Here in this realm where cold winds roam,
Every frost speaks of a secret home.
Painted memories, soft and bright,
In the depths of winter's delicate light.

Veiled Truths of a Cold Mind

Behind the shield, a stillness lies,
Veiled truths hidden from searching eyes.
Cold thoughts echo, a muted song,
Whispering doubts where few belong.

In shadows deep, intentions blur,
Silent screams, feelings stir and purr.
Fragments of warmth, like stars they fade,
Truths entwined in the doubts we've made.

A heart encased, wrapped tight in ice,
Searching for warmth, yet paying the price.
Veils of reason, so carefully spun,
Masking the chaos from life's cruel run.

Yet in the depths, a flicker glows,
A spark that whispers what the heart knows.
Beneath the ice, the longing waits,
For thawing moments to open gates.

In cold reflections, we find our way,
Through veiled truths that guide our stay.
For even in darkness, hope can bind,
The fragmented pieces of a cold mind.

Winter's Heartbeat in Silence

In stillness of night, winter sighs,
Heartbeat echoes beneath moonlit skies.
Soft as a whisper, flakes drift down,
Cloaking the world in a silvery gown.

Silence reigns, a sacred space,
Embracing the chill with gentle grace.
Each flake carries stories of old,
Whispers of warmth in the icy cold.

Bare branches stretch, reaching for light,
In the hush of snow, dreams take flight.
Winter's song, a lullaby sweet,
Dancing shadows beneath frozen feet.

In the heart of the frost, time slows to feel,
Memories wrap like a soothing reel.
With every heartbeat, the stillness breathes,
Life's simple truths in winter's eaves.

In the quiet, the soul finds peace,
In winter's embrace, worries cease.
For within the silence, we hear the call,
Winter's heartbeat, the heart of it all.

The Frostbitten Mind

Thoughts freeze in icy air,
Whispers lost in winter's chill.
Memories wrapped in despair,
Echoes linger, linger still.

Fractured dreams like frost on glass,
Silent screams and quiet sighs.
In the stillness, shadows pass,
Time's cruel grasp, a chilling rise.

With each breath, a crystal glaze,
Haunting moments, crystal clear.
Lost within this frozen maze,
Every heartbeat frozen near.

Snowflakes dance, a ghostly waltz,
Carving stories in the night.
In the cold, no one exalts,
Frostbitten thoughts take their flight.

Underneath the chilly sky,
A flicker of warmth, a spark.
With a sigh, the heart will try,
To break free from winter's dark.

Blankets of Tranquility

Softly falls the velvet snow,
Covering the world in white.
Nature's touch, a gentle flow,
Blanketing all through the night.

In this quiet, time stands still,
All the chaos fades away.
Peace descends, a soothing thrill,
In the night, the quiet sway.

Footsteps crunch on frosty trails,
Whispers dance with winds that sing.
In the stillness, hope prevails,
Winter's grip, a tender thing.

Stars illuminate the dark,
Guiding hearts through cold embrace.
In the silence, find your spark,
Journey forth, a slower pace.

Wrapped in layers, soft and warm,
Find your solace in the glow.
Tranquility, a soothing charm,
In these blankets, love will flow.

Frozen Fancies

Icicles crown the window's ledge,
Winter's breath, a crystal dream.
Eyes adorned with frost's own edge,
In this world, all feels extreme.

Whispers stir the frozen air,
Every flicker turns to ice.
In your gaze, the frosty flare,
Frozen fancies, cool and nice.

Wandering through the winter's gleam,
Imaginations take their flight.
Caught within a sparkling beam,
Fleeting glances in the night.

Shadows dance on snow's white face,
Silent tales of love and loss.
Every step, a fleeting trace,
Haunt the paths where memories toss.

In the chill, a warmth unfolds,
Fantasy shines through the frost.
Frozen stories, soft and bold,
In this realm, we are not lost.

Glacial Contemplations

Thoughts drift like snowflakes slow,
Landing softly on the ground.
In this peace, the mind will flow,
Silence deepens all around.

Reflections near the icy stream,
Ripples cause a soft displace.
In the stillness, find the dream,
Contemplations take their space.

Time moves like a glacier's path,
Slow but steady, ever clear.
In the quiet, feel the math,
Every moment, drawn near.

Beneath the surface, life awaits,
Hidden treasures, deeply sown.
In the cold, the heart creates,
Words unspoken, gently grown.

Listen close to winter's breath,
Gather thoughts, let worries fade.
In the chill, find life in death,
Glacial ways, a peace conveyed.

Hushed Resilience Amidst the Freeze

In the cold night, whispers dwell,
Each flake tells a tale to tell.
Branches swayed, still they remain,
Silent strength through winter's bane.

Shadows cast beneath the light,
Stars emerge, a dance so slight.
Roots dig deep in frozen ground,
Holding on, though silence found.

Crystal skies, a world anew,
Embers glow in quiet hue.
Though the chill wants to confine,
Hope ignites, like burning wine.

Frosted breath reveals the fight,
Resilience blooms in starry night.
Every challenge, every test,
Courage rises, never rest.

Through the ice, the heart beats strong,
In the stillness, we belong.
Nature's voice, a song of grace,
Hushed resilience we embrace.

A Dance with the Frosty Muse

Underneath the silver moon,
Frosty whispers start to croon.
Dancing lights, a gleaming stream,
Every moment feels like a dream.

Footsteps soft on glistening ground,
In this world, magic is found.
Swirling flakes paint stories bright,
Embraced in winter's chilly light.

The chilly breeze, a playful sigh,
Guide my heart to soar and fly.
With each step, my spirit's free,
Lost in this frosty reverie.

Twirls and leaps in crystalline air,
Joyful heart, without a care.
Nature twirls, a frozen show,
In this dance, I come alive, glow.

When the dawn begins to break,
In the warmth, the world will wake.
Yet in my soul, the lessons burn,
For the frost, I shall always yearn.

Mermaids Beneath the Frozen Sea

Beneath the ice, the mermaids sing,
Echoes of secrets they gently bring.
Glistening scales in cold embrace,
Adventure dwells in a hidden place.

Silent realms beneath the frost,
In crystal caves, no soul is lost.
Whispers of waves, a gentle hum,
Calling the brave to overcome.

With shimmering tails, they glide so free,
Guardians of ancient mystery.
Each frosty bubble tells a tale,
Where magic and wonder prevail.

In this kingdom, time stands still,
Hearts entwined with ocean's will.
Secrets veiled in icy blue,
Mermaids dwell where few pursue.

Through the storms and tempests' roar,
Their strength is woven at the core.
Beneath the ice, a vibrant spark,
Alive beneath the tranquil dark.

Traces of Ice in a Warm Heart

In a heart that beats so warm,
Traces of ice, a unique charm.
Memories linger, cold yet bright,
Fractured moments in soft twilight.

Winter's touch on tender veins,
Familiar comforts, sweet refrains.
With every breath, the warmth does rise,
Through frozen depths, my spirit flies.

Fires within ignite the day,
Chasing every chill away.
Yet in the stillness, ice remains,
Whispering truths amidst the gains.

Balance found in the dance of time,
In shadows deep, we learn to climb.
The warmth expands, envelops tight,
Embracing traces of the night.

In the heart, the seasons shift,
Melting ice, a precious gift.
Holding on to light and spark,
From icy whispers, love ignites.

The Stillness of Winter's Muse

In quiet woods, the shadows creep,
Where whispers blend, the night is deep.
Soft breath of frost on branches bare,
Nature holds secrets in the air.

A blanket white wraps all in peace,
As time stands still, and worries cease.
Each flake a story, softly spun,
In the glow of dusk, the day is done.

Stillness speaks in silent tones,
Where snowflakes dance on ancient stones.
The world is hushed, a sacred space,
Winter's muse, in cold embrace.

Footprints marked on crystal floors,
Lead to wonders behind closed doors.
In this stillness, dreams take flight,
Wrapped in the arms of gentle night.

With every breath, the air is clear,
The heart can listen, the soul can hear.
A tender moment, fleeting, bright,
In winter's hush, we find our light.

Echoes in the Snowlight

Beneath the stars, the world aglow,
Echoes linger in the snow.
Whispers weave through chilly air,
Carried softly, everywhere.

Footsteps crunch on glistening ground,
Nature's silence is profound.
Moonbeams dance on frosty pines,
In this realm where magic shines.

Hearts unite in winter's song,
In the stillness, we belong.
Echoes of laughter fill the night,
As snowflakes fall, pure and white.

Candles flicker in warm embrace,
Lighting paths through every space.
Stories shared by fireside glow,
Memories linger in the snow.

Time stands still as shadows play,
In winter's charms, we wish to stay.
With every breath, we feel the cheer,
In echoes, love draws ever near.

Secrets Buried in the Drift

Beneath the snow, where shadows lie,
Secrets whisper, time slips by.
Layers soft, like dreams concealed,
Nature's magic is revealed.

In frosty drifts, the stories blend,
Of moments lost, yet never end.
The chill embraces hearts aglow,
In the quiet, we come to know.

Each flake that falls, a tale to tell,
In icy realms where echoes dwell.
Beneath the white, the warmth resides,
Lost in winter, our love abides.

Whispers linger in the breeze,
Carried soft through winter trees.
Every step breaks through the cold,
In this journey, we grow bold.

Secrets linger, waiting so,
In the heart of winter's glow.
A drift of dreams, pure and bright,
Hiding truths in soft moonlight.

Glistening Memories on Silent Streets

In the hush of night, a world aglow,
Glistening streets, where soft winds blow.
Footsteps echo, a tender sound,
In winter's embrace, love is found.

Each streetlight flickers, casting dreams,
Illuminating our silent schemes.
Memories sparkle, bright and clear,
On paths where joy and hope appear.

A distant laughter fills the air,
As shadows dance, we find our share.
In every corner, whispers stay,
Glistening moments that will not fray.

Snowflakes weave through tales of old,
In every drift, our hearts unfold.
Reflecting warmth in biting cold,
Silent streets, where stories are told.

In the chill of night, we roam free,
Inspired by what we see.
Glistening memories softly greet,
In winter's magic, we feel complete.

Frost-Kissed Memories from the Past

In the quiet dawn, where shadows play,
Whispers of snowflakes gently sway.
Halls of laughter echo in the cold,
Frost-kissed dreams that never grow old.

Images dance on icy panes,
Childhood wishes, soft refrains.
Each breath a cloud, a story untold,
In the warmth of memory, we both hold.

Footprints trace the paths we've crossed,
Moments cherished, never lost.
With every chill that bites the skin,
A rush of joy lies deep within.

The world outside, a crystal blaze,
Reflects the glow of our golden days.
Wrapped in warmth, we share a sigh,
In every flake, our hearts comply.

Frost-kissed nights under starry skies,
Where glistening dreams surely arise.
In the silence, love's echoes ring,
And memories dance on winter's wing.

Layers of Frosted Reverie

In the depth of night, a hush descends,
The world is cloaked, as stillness lends.
Layers of frost on branches cling,
Nature's beauty in slumbering spring.

A blanket white on the ground below,
Whispers of warmth in the chill winds blow.
Time frozen still in a delicate trance,
As snowflakes swirl in a fleeting dance.

Pages of dreams tucked under snow,
Visions of warmth in the shadows glow.
Every flake a secret shared,
In layers thick, our hearts have bared.

Beneath the frost, life waits in peace,
Hopes held tight, never to cease.
In the stillness, we find our way,
Through layers of night into the day.

A tapestry woven of memory's thread,
Each glistening bead, a tale we've said.
In frozen moments where love has grown,
Layers of joy in the heart's soft stone.

Winter's Canvas of Unspoken Yearnings

Under the hush of a snowy veil,
A canvas wide, where dreams set sail.
Brushstrokes of white, pure and bright,
Painting wishes in the quiet night.

Dreams wrapped tight in frost's embrace,
Each twinkle glows, a gentle grace.
In the chill, our spirits soar,
Yearning whispers at winter's door.

With every flake, a wish takes flight,
Carried away by the frosty night.
Softly falling, they drift and sway,
On winter's canvas, hopes will play.

Silent wishes in the evening light,
Glowing embers, warm and bright.
Under pale moons, our hearts remain,
Fueling the fire in the cold disdain.

Caught in dreams of a summer's song,
In the silence, we know we belong.
With every snowflake that graces the ground,
The echoes of love in the stillness found.

Calms of Ice and Reflective Thought

In the stillness where shadows rest,
Clarity blooms, a heart at best.
Calms of ice in the deepening night,
Guiding thoughts in the soft moonlight.

Frozen rivers of tranquil grace,
Reflective moments in this quiet space.
Nature's breath, a gentle pause,
In every stillness, a noble cause.

Fractured light on a crystal sea,
Rays of hope effortlessly free.
Within the quiet, reflections unfold,
Unspoken truths in the crisp and cold.

Here in the calm, where silence breathes,
A tapestry spun from winter's leaves.
Thoughts meander on icy trails,
Carried softly on the whispering gales.

In this stillness, I find my way,
Through the maze of night to day.
With every thought that drifts and glides,
In the calm of ice, my spirit bides.

Unraveled Dreams of the Frozen

In the stillness of night, dreams lay bare,
Whispers of frost weave through the air.
Silent shadows dance on the snow,
Echoes of hopes that long ago flow.

Fractured wishes in icy streams,
Illuminated softly, like fading beams.
Hearts once warm now frozen tight,
Craving the warmth of a distant light.

In the cradle of winter's hand,
Unraveled threads softly stand.
A tapestry of yesteryears,
Interwoven with long lost tears.

Beneath the stars, a story unfolds,
In the chill of night, memories hold.
Each breath a cloud, drifting wide,
Shrouded in dreams where secrets bide.

Frosted paths lead to unknown ways,
Through the maze of forgotten days.
With every heartbeat, a chance to find,
The warmth of dreams intertwined.

Celestial Patterns in Winter's Air

As the heavens stretch vast and deep,
Winter's breath stirs from its sleep.
Stars adorn the silent sky,
A tapestry where the snowflakes lie.

Patterns dance in the cool night breeze,
Cosmic whispers among the trees.
Galaxies spiral, bright and clear,
Drawing the dreams of all who near.

Each flake a note in a soft refrain,
Symphonies played through the winter rain.
Celestial maps hang overhead,
Guiding the hearts where the lost have tread.

Beneath the chill, warmth still glows,
In every breath, the mystery grows.
Winter's canvas kissed by stars,
Ink of the night, our guiding memoirs.

Here in the stillness, hope takes flight,
Celestial patterns spark the night.
Dreamers gather, lost in wonder,
Embracing the magic pulled asunder.

Enchanted by the Crystal Flakes

Falling softly, the world is shy,
Crystal flakes in the twilight sky.
Each one a gem, uniquely spun,
Whispers of frost when day is done.

Caught in the glow of the silver moon,
Flakes dance lightly, a gentle tune.
Around each corner, magic weaves,
Lighting the paths where the heart believes.

In the hush, a symphony plays,
As winter deepens its loving gaze.
Secrets glisten on every ledge,
Promises kept by the frozen edge.

A world transformed, a fairy tale,
In every flake, a whispered gale.
With every touch, enchantment grows,
Rooted in love as the cold wind blows.

Embraced by winter's soft, sweet grace,
We find our warmth in a crystal space.
Holding dreams that in silence flutter,
Eternally bound in the softest utter.

Tranquil Visions Under Winter's Glow

Underneath the silver night,
Winter casts its tranquil light.
Softly glimmers on the ground,
A peaceful hush all around.

In this stillness, time gives way,
Echoes of dreams from yesterday.
Each breath a whisper, calm and clear,
In winter's arms, we draw so near.

The moon a guardian, softly bright,
Nurturing hearts in the quiet night.
With every sigh, the world slows down,
Beneath the stars, we wear a crown.

Snowflakes twinkle like distant stars,
Cradling hopes that heal our scars.
In their descent, stories swirl,
Wrapping our souls in a gentle twirl.

Tranquil visions take their flight,
Illuminated in winter's light.
In this moment, the heart takes root,
Finding solace in the absolute.

Veils of Winter's Embrace

In the hush of falling flakes,
Whispers dance on frosty air.
Nature dons her silver gown,
Shadows linger everywhere.

Branches bow with crystal weight,
Silence wraps the world so tight.
Footsteps crunch on hidden trails,
Guided by the soft moonlight.

The fire flickers warm and bright,
Chasing chills that seek to stay.
Hot cocoa warms our gentle hands,
As night fades into sparkling day.

With each breath, a cloud appears,
Breath of winter, brave and bold.
In the night, the stars play games,
Their stories silently told.

Hold my heart within this space,
Veils of winter, soft and pure.
In the stillness, life awaits,
Wrapped in peace, forever sure.

Crystal Reflections at Dusk

Twilight paints the skies in hues,
Of gentle blues and fiery reds.
The world reflects in shards of glass,
As daylight slowly ebbs and spreads.

Mirrored lakes embrace the sky,
Each ripple sings a soft refrain.
Whispers of the coming night,
Echo through the quiet lane.

Crickets chirp their evening song,
As stars awaken one by one.
Crystal dewdrops on the grass,
Sparkle in the dusk's soft run.

We stroll along this mirrored path,
In search of dreams that twinkle bright.
Lost in thoughts, we softly laugh,
As shadows dance and take their flight.

In the stillness, hearts align,
Mirrored souls beneath the stars.
Crystal reflections intertwine,
In the dusk, where beauty is ours.

A Frosted Silence Descends

A blanket of frost covers all,
In silence, the world seems to sigh.
Each flake falls like whispered dreams,
Beneath the vast and starry sky.

Trees adorned in icy lace,
Stand guard 'gainst the midnight bold.
Every whisper holds a secret,
In the chill, where truths unfold.

Footprints fade upon the ground,
Memories lost in winter's spell.
Shadows mingle, softly bound,
In the silence, we dwell.

The moon peeks from behind the clouds,
Casting silver on the snow.
A frosted silence wraps us close,
In a world where time moves slow.

Embrace this moment, sweet and still,
Let your heart be free and light.
In the beauty of the frosted night,
Find your peace, find your light.

Beneath the White Blanket

Underneath the white blanket,
Nature sleeps in soft repose.
Dreams are cradled, gently tucked,
As winter's chill brings silent prose.

The world is hushed, the air is pure,
As time stands still, no sound to break.
Each flake a promise, soft and sure,
In this realm where spirits awake.

The stars twinkle like distant wishes,
Casting light on fervent dreams.
Beneath this cover of ice and bliss,
Life awakens, or so it seems.

An owl's call breaks the frozen air,
A reminder of nature's grace.
Beneath this white blanket we share,
The warmth of love finds a place.

Let the snowflakes fall and dance,
In this world of wonder, so bright.
Beneath the white blanket, our hearts prance,
As we find solace in the night.

Milton Keynes UK
Ingram Content Group UK Ltd.
UKHW010228111224
452348UK00011B/589